UnKindled

Yusuf Kiser

BookLeaf Publishing

India | USA | UK

Presentation by *BookLeaf Publishing*

Web: www.bookleafpub.com

E-mail: info@bookleafpub.com

Cover Art by Sana Nabeel

Instagram: @sananabeel09

@peer.flow.trainings

ISBN: 9789363303928

First edition 2024

To all who are ready for life

*A fire burns within... the flames of an
inconsolable passion.*

*A passion for change. For enjoyment. For
companionship. And for freedom. Freedom from
the fear of a life unlived...*

PREFACE

So, this book I decided to write very quickly, actually. It was off of the back of a TV show I had just finished filming a few days prior. As a committed writer, I'm used to writing every day, so when I saw an ad for a 21-day writing challenge, I jumped at the opportunity. Not only because I enjoy writing, but also because I'm very competitive—and the idea of doing a publication time trial was incredibly exciting...

Coming off of a very pivotal moment in my life, I decided to channel my creative flow by writing 1 or 2 poems a day, whenever I felt inspired—leaving the innate day-to-day feelings splattered on each page. The goal was to capture the raw emotions I felt during the days after igniting a crucial step in my own self-actualization and package it so that you and many others can draw inspiration from it. With that said, I hope you enjoy, my friend...

Hiding Light

Why do you hide?
You know your path is right

Why do you hide?
And say you want the light

Why do you hide?
Conceal what's in your mind

Why do you hide?
In fear of wrong or right

Why do you hide?
Perhaps it's just as easy

Why do you hide?
To float on by in silence

Why do you hide?
Perhaps it's not as easy

Why do you hide?
To face your soulful violence

In the Wake of Dreams

In the wake of endless dreams
We find out truly what they mean...

What the heart desires...
And what it Leaves to find it

The path untraveled hurts
But not knowing pains much more

What could have been may yet still be
Once you claim what's yours

A Turn of Fate

As the world turns, keep your chin
level
For where it lands may surprise you

Who can know which side will win?
Just let your spirit guide you

Careful now; these stairs have nails
A fall from you they seek

But as you climb, just know one thing
Speak true that which you seek

An Echo of the Future

An echo of a past remembered
Dust begins to settle

To rediscover who you are
The winds of change must blow

A fallacy of truth behooves you
But listen—you do not

Now it's you who holds the keys
To the future that you sought

The Space Between

In a world full of whispers
The quiet mind sings

Drawing on peace
From the space in between

The darkness is loud
Yet the light shines in silence

What a beautiful thing
Not to heed to lost guidance

The Hunt

In the eyes of the sheep
A wolf appears weak

In the eyes of the deer
A hunter draws near

Each step, a crunch
But never too loud

Just one blink
And the sheep starts to prowl

On the brink of Greatness

With great speed, the needle drops
Leaving room for but a breath

Keep up, says the spirit
Knowing fate will weave and weft

Quickly now, you're almost there
Like a child, you contest

Soon you'll see the prize you've won
And smile while you rest

The Flow of Choice

Choices dance in the shallow river
Close, but ever far

To reach a hand is to commit
But not decide with eyes ajar

A flinch ensures the vision stalls
To reach too much could haste the fall

Patience breathes. A life will live
Untempted by the call

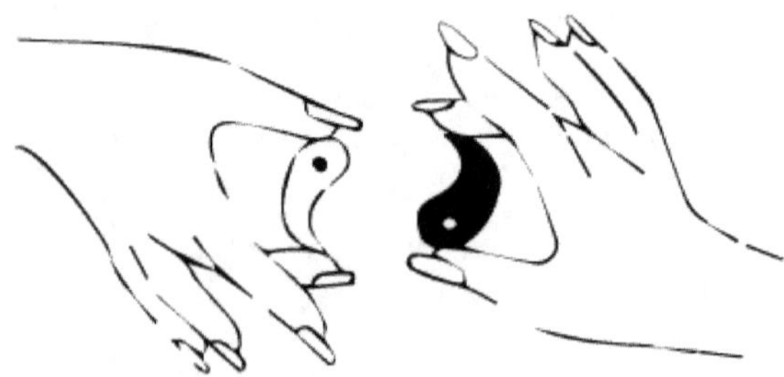

The Eternal Heart

Bleeding heart. The stitches sewn
Inside you'll find the needle

As crimson trickles down your chest
You'll find resistance feeble

A voice calls to let it flow
It says, "don't be afraid"

And once you do, you'll feel no pain
You'll always be okay

A Life of Green

What say you, child
To the bare bones of a withered tree,
pining to be filled with leaves?

A whispered word of hollow thoughts?
We'll see what morning sunlight brings

The day is young so seize it well
—Each one goes tick by tick

But listen now; consider this
What from each tick you'll get

A Kindred Calm

In the depth of night, The long wind
crawls
Lade with wisps of calm...

What once Was—is once again
Brought on by other calls

A kindred soul, once feeling lost
Searching for a friend

A friend was found and with some
luck
They'll feel love once again

The Luck that's Made

Now the day turns over dusk
Searching yet again

A crushing pain befalls the heart
And will not yield in vain

If only moments tip the scale
Why wait for simple luck

If luck you get's the luck you make
Then make it heart untucked

A Distant Flame

A spark ignites a distant flame
A friend of time sought once again

Within their dreams, they've shared a
bond
Eyes of wealth, with measure beyond

And though that dream had started
young
A song of time, the notes they've sung

Climbing, reaching, for the goal
Before gray hairs and bones grow old

A Sharp Resolve

If this then that, If tit then tat
Forth back the pendulum swings

Only time partitions weight
And "wait" a calm heart brings

Don't wait too long; the iron's hot
So steel your sharp resolve

And when it's time to follow through
You'll know which move to call

The Walls Within

A whole night follows the wind
A whole night goes unwasted

Sounds of desire fill thyne ear
As lightning strikes more places

A bellowed breath... anticipation
The night's troubles spread thin

If only one could rise above
The handmade walls within

At The Speed of Life

A quickened pace, a lightened step
A joyful hum in triumph

The work not done has yet been won
Watch coals turn full to diamonds

Rest now; the night is young
You'll need your strength come
morrow

And trust that once the day is done
You'll not come home in sorrow

The Hearts of Giants

Eyes set forward, smile cracked
The deed is almost done

One-day wins are common ground
The limit, set to none

Don't look past a common sheep
They're you but you looked over

In every heart, there lives a heap
Of stones made out of boulders

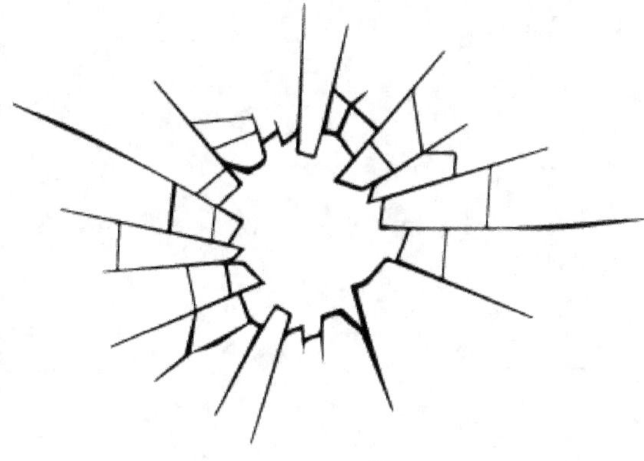

Boundless Gratitude

The long night sings, A wisp of love
Now, we sit in silence.

Oh blissful dawn, Warm rays connect
A resting soul sheds violence

Hear me now, oh joyous one
Your time is truly treasured

For hearts will fill, and tears will flow
With Gratitude unmeasured

The Tree of Life

Light turns, a pulsing beat
The flow is unimpeded

With a solemn breath, it's written
The folds of life now pleated

A precious nugget of wisdom found
Cradled in the palm

The best is yet to come, they say
And with it, leaves will fall

Dreams with Steam

A brightened spark ignites the flame
Of life from once before

A hearty laugh of friendship rings
Ego now dropped at the door

A world of love is shared between
A flash to once-held hopes and dreams

Never truly given up
But watered just to make the steam

The Flame within

A walk through sand, grains they shift
Footprints break the mold

It's not until a step within
That each one takes it's hold

Leap again, unburdened breath
Your story might surprise you

Like flowers bloom in weary depths
The fire burns inside you

End of Book "Author's Challenge"

And so, my friend... now I ask you. Actually, I challenge you too to write a few poems, goals, dreams, plans—or anything of your choosing for the remainder of this book. I'm a believer in the fact that our words have the power to cause great change in our lives, so if you feel inspired, let this be a kindle to your life's flame—whether already ignited or just starting to spark. I hope you've enjoyed this because from here it's your turn... Good luck, my friend... Much Love.

24

Acknowledgments

I'd like to shout out to all my friends and family who have loved and supported me on any and every part of my journey—I legitimately wouldn't be where I am now without you guys, and certainly not in as good condition.

And I want to give a special shout-out to my mother—not only for everything you've done in raising me, but in relation to me writing this book...

I remember how you used to read books to me at night or whenever things would be tough, and I remember one poem in particular that became one of my favorites—"Mother to Son" by Langston Hughes. So along with the theme of that poem, I want to say thank you for not sitting down on those stairs and for helping inspire me not to as well. I appreciate you a lot, and I hope you've enjoyed these words 😌 🙏 🖤

Let's Stay in Touch

Hello my friend, and thank you for reading. I hope it's served you well. If you'd like to see more of my work or connect with me, reach out on any of my social media, and I'll be glad to share some love. 🖤 And if you will, please leave a review on the platform you purchased on, and share it with a friend or family member. I'd love to hear your thoughts—and it helps my work reach more people.

Until next time... much love

Website:
http://beacons.ai/dreamdrivebooks
Instagram: @dreamdrivepoetry
@hakeem_kiser
Twitter: Hakeem_Kiser
Blue Sky: HakeemKiser.bsky.social
TikTok: @dreamdrivepublishing
LinkedIn: Hakeem Kiser
Facebook: DreamDrive Books